GREAT PERFORMER'S EDITION

NATHAN MILSTEIN

Three Transcriptions

for Violin and Piano

ED 3082

ISBN 0-7935-5463-2

G. SCHIRMER, Inc.

DISTRIBUTED BY

HAL•LEONARD®
CORPORATION

7777 W. BLUEMOUND RD. P.O. BOX 13819 MILWAUKEE, WI 53213

Nocturne

Frédéric Chopin
(Posthumous)
Transcribed by Nathan Milstein

Lullaby
from: Mazeppa

Piotr Ilyitch Tchaikovsky
Transcribed by Nathan Milstein

Violin

GREAT PERFORMER'S EDITION

NATHAN MILSTEIN

Three Transcriptions

for Violin and Piano

ED 3082

ISBN 0-7935-5463-2

G. SCHIRMER, Inc.

DISTRIBUTED BY

HAL•LEONARD®
CORPORATION

7777 W. BLUEMOUND RD. P.O. BOX 13819 MILWAUKEE, WI 53213

Nocturne

Violin

Frédéric Chopin
(Posthumous)
Transcribed by Nathan Milstein

48101c

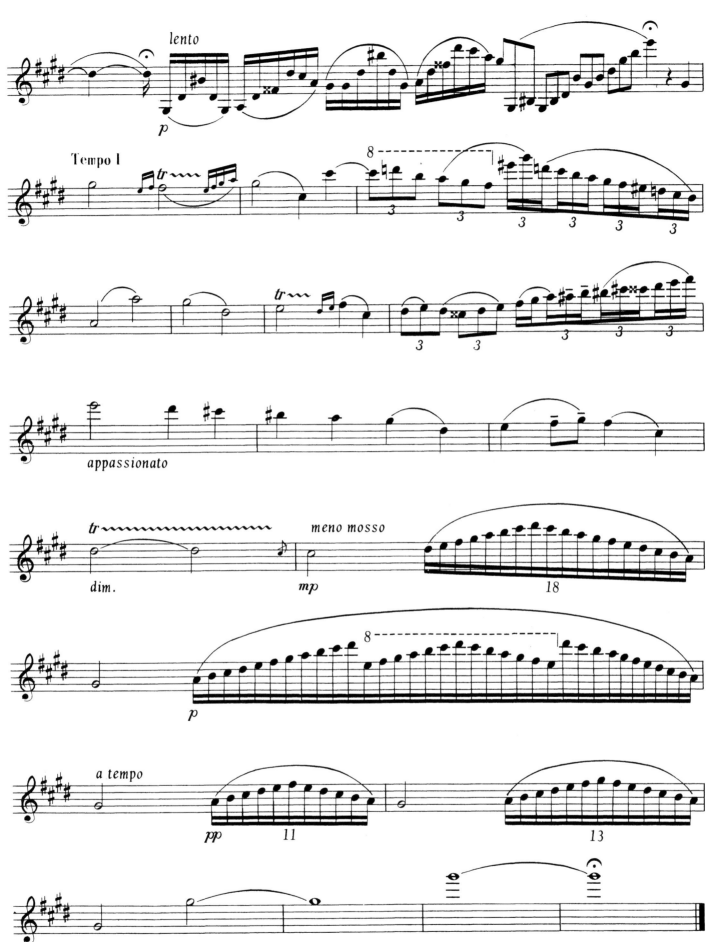

Lullaby
from : Mazeppa

Violin

Piotr Ilyitch Tchaikovsky
Transcribed by Nathan Milstein

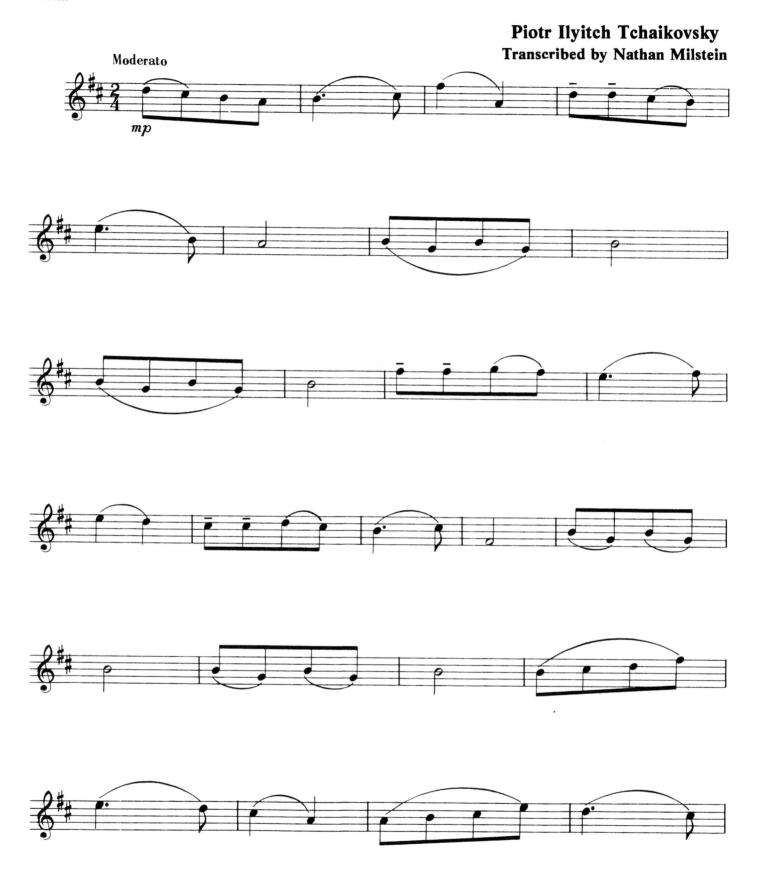

48101c

Consolation

Violin

Franz Liszt
Transcribed by Nathan Milstein

48101c

Consolation

Franz Liszt
Transcribed by Nathan Milstein

48101c